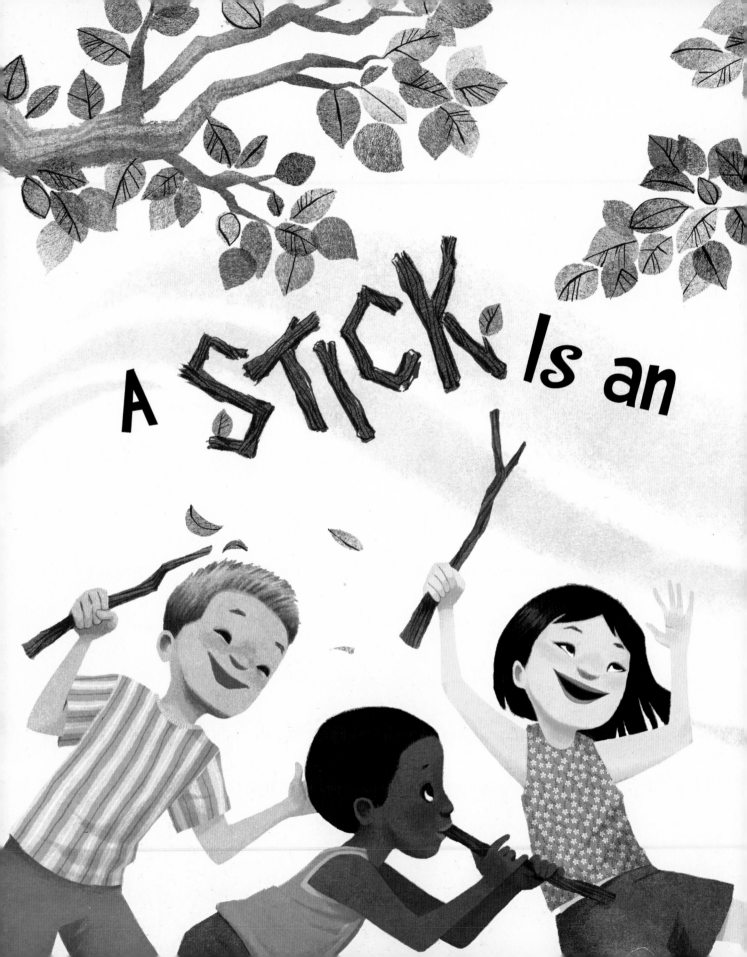

A Stick Is an

EXCELLENT THING

Poems Celebrating Outdoor Play

BY

Marilyn Singer

ILLUSTRATED BY

LeUyen Pham

Clarion Books
Houghton Mifflin Harcourt
Boston New York 2012

FIRST ONE OUT

Every summer morning
I'm always the first one
to go outside, to toss my ball,
to lose it in the sun.

Today my poodle finds it
in Mom's strawberry patch,
then turns the game I played alone
into rounds of catch.

EDGES

I like to walk the edges—
    the curbs, the rims, the little ledges.
I am careful not to tilt,
    to stumble, slump, or wilt.
        I pay attention to my feet
           so that every step is neat.
        I am dancing in the air,
           but I never leave the street.

REALLY FAST!

Skateboard races,
   pigeon chases,
      running bases.
Backyard dashes,
   racecar crashes,
      puddle splashes.

Everything's a blast
when you do it really fast!

JACKS

A flick of the wrist,
a really quick scoop,
a dozen at once
    from the top of the stoop.
I'm the boss of the toss,
so you cannot relax.
When you play with me,
    I'm the queen of the jacks.

BUBBLES

This bubble I'm blowing,
this bubble is growing—
this bubble of ginormous size.
It's as big as a plate.
You can watch it inflate.
This bubble will win me a prize!
This bubble I'm blowing,
this bubble keeps growing—
this bubble does not want to stop.
It's as big as a planet.
Can't get bigger—or can it?
This bubble will never go . . .
POP!

My brother likes to boast
he can blow the biggest bubbles.
Yes, but I can blow the most.
So I'm hiding in the shade,
where it's cool and he can't see
who is sending this parade
of small bubbles—a whole fleet—
that is sailing right behind him
up the steamy summer street.

JUMP!

In the town
      town
        town
          there are noises all around.

      Come on, listen
          listen
            listen
      to my favorite sidewalk sound!

How Do You Like to Swing?

How do you like to swing?
> Straight up and straight down?
> In a circle, round and round?
> Near the sky or near the ground?

How do you like to swing?
> On your belly? On your seat?
> Do you ask for a push?
> Do you use your own feet?

How do you like to swing?
> Wide-eyed or dreaming?
> Do you sometimes sing a song?
> Do you pump for just five minutes?

Could you swing the whole day long?

MONKEY IN THE MIDDLE

Hey, hey, diddle, diddle!
There's no time to twiddle
your thumbs or twirl your hair
when you're the Monkey in the Middle.

Don't stop to scratch an itch.
Don't ever try to fiddle
with your hat or underwear
when you're the Monkey in the Middle.

How do you win the game?
That's no big riddle!
Pluck that ball from the air.
There you go—fair and square!

Now another kid's the Monkey in the Middle!

Upside Down

Upside-down houses
  with upside-down stoops.
  Upside-down players
  at upside-down hoops.
  Upside-down sparrows
  in upside-down trees,
  clinging to twigs
  in an upside-down breeze.
  Upside-down strollers
  and upside-down cars.
  And upside-down me
  on the high monkey bars.

SPRINKLER

Chilly twinkler.

Water sprinkler.

Big drops flash.

Hurry, dash!

You can enter

through the center.

Or just wait,
standing straight.

Let that spray
head your way.

Get wet! Jump out!

And always SHOUT!

STATUES

We don't play Statues like other kids do.

    The Sculptor (that's me) grabs the Clay (that's you),

spins in wide circles, swings and swings

you fast and faster. Then—whoosh!—she flings,

    and yells out, *Freeze!* No one can budge

    while she walks around and gets to judge.

The winner is her favorite pose.
Again! Till someone grabs the hose

and with a holler, starts to spray.
Bye-bye, Sculptor! So long, Clay!

Water-fight finish! Everyone melts.
We don't play Statues like anyone else.

HIDE-AND-SEEK

One, two, three, uh-uh, you can't see me
behind this willow tree.
I stand here oh so still,
pretend I'm in Brazil,
where lots of birds fly free
and silent snakes go gliding.
That's right—I'm good at hiding!

Ready or not, first I'm cold, then I'm hot.
I swear I'm gonna spot
you standing over there.
You haven't got a prayer.
We play this game a lot,
so you know I'm not peeking.
I'm just too good at seeking!

Making Soup

Soup, soup, we're making soup
    with grass and stones and mud (one scoop),
      a hunk of cheese, a celery stalk,
      an old cigar, a piece of chalk.
We stir it with a ballpoint pen,
      then throw it out and start again.

BARRELING

This hill is small. The grass feels fluffy.
Mama says it's called a *knoll.*
We're glad our clothes are old and scruffy.
When we go down, we never stroll—
we roll!

HOPSCOTCH

Got a dime?

> Got a penny.
> Got some chalk?

I've got plenty.
I'll make squares,
  one through eight.

> Hurry up! I can't wait!
> I can hop like a bunny.

On four legs?

> Don't be funny!

You just stepped on a line.
It's my turn.

> Okay. Fine.
> Whoop, whoop—both feet down!
> My turny-burny.

You're a clown!

> Seven, eight,
> Paris, Rome.
> Turn around,
> hop, hop home.

Watch *me* now!
Three, two, one.
Jump on out!
Now I'm done!

We rock!
Best hopscotchers
on the block!

We're really good.

We really rock!

We're good!
Best hopscotchers
in the 'hood!

27

A Stick Is an Excellent Thing

A stick is an excellent thing.
If you find the perfect one,
it's a scepter for a king.
A stick is an excellent thing.

It's a magic wand. It's yours to fling,
to strum a fence, to draw the sun.
A stick is an excellent thing
if you find the perfect one.

CATCHING FIREFLIES

Fireflies don't bother me.
Fireflies don't scare me.
They never bite; they just make light.
I'll catch some, if you dare me!

I'll put them in a big glass jar.
We'll watch them flash and glow
for a minute or two, then so long, toodle-oo!
It's time to let them go.

STARGAZING

Looking at the summer stars
    is our latest game.
I like to count them one by one
    while Dad gives each a name.

He says it's so much better
    than trying to count sheep.
We make the stars our very own
    before we fall asleep.

To Lynne, Hazel, and Jesse,
who like to go out and play
—M.S.

To Kavi and Sabine
—L.P.

Clarion Books
215 Park Avenue South
New York, New York 10003

Text copyright © 2012 by Marilyn Singer
Illustrations copyright © 2012 by LeUyen Pham

The text of this book is set in 16-point Triplex Serif.
The art for this book was rendered in pencil and ink, then colored digitally.
"Making Soup" first appeared in *Climb Inside a Poem* by Georgia Heard and Lester Laminack. Portsmouth, N.H.: Firsthand/Heineman, 2007.
"Stargazing" first appeared in *Here's a Little Poem* by Jane Yolen and Andrew Fusek Peters. London: Walker, 2007.

Clarion Books is an imprint of Houghton Mifflin Harcourt Publishing Company.

www.hmhbooks.com

Library of Congress Cataloging-in-Publication Data
Singer, Marilyn.
A stick is an excellent thing : poems celebrating outdoor play / by Marilyn Singer ; illustrated by LeUyen Pham.
p. cm.
ISBN 978-0-547-12493-3
I. Outdoor recreation—Juvenile poetry. I. Pham, LeUyen, ill. II. Title.
PS3569.I546S75 2012
811'.54—dc22
2011009848

Manufactured in China
LEO 10 9 8 7 6 5 4 3 2 1
4500331192